270

THE S____
ATHEIST'S GUIDE
to Mystical Experiences
(and how to have them)

SOREN SORENSEN

Published by Spiral Garden

Published by Spiral Garden
www.SpiralGarden.com

ISBN: 978-0-9858237-2-6

First Edition
Published January 2020

DEDICATION

This book is dedicated to all that is,
all that has been, and all that will ever be.

May we all experience ever-greater happiness forever!

To this end, a portion of all proceeds will be used to establish
and nurture the Center for a Better World and its projects.
www.CenterForABetterWorld.com

CONTENTS

ACKNOWLEDGMENTS

I would like to acknowledge and appreciate, with the whole of my being, all past, present, and future wisdom teachers, both celebrated and forgotten, who have offered a portion of their lives to share the essence of what I, too, attempt to share within these pages. It has never been an easy or welcome task, as one must encounter the inertia of ignorance. Fortunately, it seems as though a worldwide awakening is *finally* near at hand!

CHAPTER 1

INTRODUCTION

"Row, row, row your boat; *gently* down the stream.
Merrily merrily, merrily, merrily; *life is but a dream.*"

A Quick Quiz *(Just for fun!)*

1) Do you believe in the existence of an entity who
allegedly exists outside of the universe and who
allegedly created and rules the universe?
(Imagine a white bearded wizard!)

2) Do you recognize the intrinsic infinite
"connectedness" and "oneness" of all things?

3) Do you *try* to live in a way that nurtures the health
and happiness of all things?

If you answered NO, YES, YES...

YOU ARE A SPIRITUAL ATHEIST!

"Spiritual Atheism" is a *classification* that I proposed (via The Center for a Better World) to exist alongside "Theism" and "Atheism". Just as there are many different forms of Theism (such as Christianity and Judaism), there are many different forms of Spiritual Atheism (such as Pantheism and Buddhism). As someone interested in this topic, it is very likely that your own beliefs, theories, and speculations about existence create a personal philosophy that is a form of Spiritual Atheism. Naturally, it is extremely valuable to carefully consider a diverse array of perspectives and philosophies as you refine your own. It is with this in mind, that I offer you a portion of my own perspective and personal philosophy.

There are three *intentional* paths to Mystical Experiences:

1) Certain Drug Use
2) Certain Extreme Physical & Mental Practices
3) Certain *Peaceful* Physical & Mental Practices

I consider drug use and extreme physical & mental practices to be both forceful and potentially dangerous paths. As such, I am not interested in them and have no experience with them. If you are interested in these particular paths, *which I do consider to be valid*, please seek genuinely experienced and trusted experts in these areas.

As for the *peaceful* path, I hope to be able to offer you authentically valuable guidance. In order to do that, I am going to tell you only what I have personally experienced and personally believe to be true. I am going to do my best to avoid assumptions, speculations, and borrowed experiences that are not explicitly disclosed as such. Even so, please keep in mind that everyone's experiences are ultimately unique and deeply influenced by one's innermost perspective, memories, beliefs, etc. Fortunately, whether or not you *precisely agree* with everything I say is *unimportant*. My words are but a finger *pointing towards* the moon (truth). *Keep your eyes on the moon!*

Similarly, the intention of this book is not to act as an *exhaustive treatise* on the various topics covered; but rather, to provide *fundamental context, clarity, and insights* that should be sufficient guidance for most people. For the rest, I am confident that the content, both revealed and concealed, within the pages of this book will make further study, if desired, far more accessible and far more effective.

As expected, this book naturally expands and builds on the information presented in my previous book, *Spiritual Atheism – The Way of Wisdom*, but I have been extremely careful to make sure that this new book is able to stand on its own, without requiring readers to (re)read my prior book first. *The two books can be read in either order!*

For this reason, there is significant redundancy (approximately 25%) between this book and my previous book, *Spiritual Atheism – The Way of Wisdom*. To be specific, most of the essential content in chapters 10-14 of my prior book has been integrated into this book. *I ask for your kind understanding.*

Similarly, there is some fundamental redundancy *within* this book, from chapter to chapter, where I deemed it necessary for the sake of better accuracy, clarity, and context. *Again, I ask for your kind understanding.*

As usual, I've attempted to write as concisely as possible. I have also attempted to write in such a way that the *subtler* content of this book will reveal itself ever more to the reader as they are ready for it. I have been told many times that my books (and other creations) seem to evolve as the reader evolves; so please don't worry if you don't fully understand, or fully appreciate, everything I say during your first reading. Just stay fully engaged where you are and know that, if you desire it, we can always meet again.

And I hope that we do!

Are you ready to learn:

> how to heal yourself and others?
> how to live peacefully and happily?
> how to get in flow and stay in flow?
> how to experience true bliss and ecstasy?
> how to know anything you want to know?
> how to manifest anything you want to manifest?

Are you ready to find out how great your life can be?

4

CHAPTER 2

WHAT IS A SPIRITUAL ATHEIST?

Although the term "Spiritual Atheist" may initially sound like an oxymoron to some, it is most definitely not. It is entirely possible to *not* believe in "God", and yet still be deeply spiritual.

Let's explore this idea a bit more.

Obviously, Spiritual Atheists do not believe in the existence of "God"; but, unfortunately, there are many different (and often ambiguous) ways in which the term "God" is currently commonly used. For this reason, it is critical that I clarify exactly what it is that Spiritual Atheists do *not* believe in. If this is not done, any inquiry such as this one will quickly become unnecessarily confused and ultimately meaningless.

For the purpose of clarifying exactly what it is that Spiritual Atheists do not believe in, "God" means "an entity who allegedly exists outside of the universe and who allegedly created and rules the universe."

I am sure that it will also be very helpful if I clarify my use of the term "the universe". In this case and context, the term "the universe" necessarily includes "everything that has ever existed, now exists, or will ever exist" (including in "parallel" or otherwise).

Now that I have explained what it is that Spiritual Atheists do *not* believe in, I can introduce the *spiritual* aspect of Spiritual Atheism.

I have been pondering the nature of spirituality for as long as I can remember. From my perspective, people tend to make this inquiry much more complicated than it actually is.

From my perspective, to be spiritual is simply to realize (consciously or unconsciously) that everything in the universe is ultimately interconnected (even if only very subtly by a cause and effect relationship over unimaginable *apparent* distances in time and space); and to think, speak, and act accordingly.

Said more simply, to be spiritual is to realize (consciously or unconsciously) that we are all infinitely and eternally interconnected (even if only by an extremely complicated cause and effect relationship); and to think, speak, and act accordingly.

It is obvious to most Spiritual Atheists that the so-called "God" that most traditional Theists worship and adore (and that most traditional Atheists reject and abhor) is actually (and ironically) a symbol (and idol) that *represents* the profound and mystical existence and nature of the universe itself. That is to say, that "God" is, in fact, a *reference* to the universe itself.

Sometimes I wonder... could it be any more obvious?

It is important to point out that if "God" was *universally* recognized as a reference to "the universe itself" (and a personal name given to it) rather than a literal and external (to the universe) being, then to be an Atheist would mean that one did not believe in the existence of the universe. Obviously, this would be a nonsensical position that would render the terms Atheist and Theist equally nonsensical. *Nonsense indeed!*

In fact, when the majority of Theists and Atheists finally do fully realize that "God" is actually a reference to the "the universe itself"; the terms Theist and Atheist (along with the actively awakening terms Non-literal Theist and Spiritual Atheist) will begin to lose their meaning, fall out of use, and ultimately become historical references only.

Much more importantly, people will begin to see existential and spiritual truth and wisdom much more easily, and begin to make ever-better choices. Said differently, people will begin to consciously polarize around genuine issues of wholistic health and disease, rather than manufactured issues that ultimately serve others' desire for profit, power, and ever-greater control at the expense of all.

Or so I hope! And I hope that day comes soon enough!

From this Spiritual Atheist's perspective, life on planet Earth is quickly being literally consumed by the results of existential and spiritual ignorance and misunderstanding.

Greed has always been a significant problem; but with our current (let alone future!) technological capabilities, it has become an *inestimable* threat. The life threatening and sobering truth is that greed is presently in control of old, new, hidden, and emerging technology; not love and wisdom. To make matters worse, the so-called "smart" people who are creating and evolving technology are not (yet) "smart enough" to stop what they are doing and consciously *help* to enlighten, liberate, unite, and empower humanity instead. (If this is you, *please* stop what you are doing and come join us instead! When love and wisdom prevails, we can again further empower and enrich ourselves with new technology; but, as it is, this is an extremely dangerous and most unwise pursuit.)

Indeed, this seems to be a very precarious time in the course of our precious planet's life, and the wisdom that Spiritual Atheism offers is desperately needed.

If you would like to explore my perspective of Spiritual Atheism in more depth, please read my previous book entitled, *Spiritual Atheism: The Way of Wisdom*. (Please note that some of that book's content is included in this book.)

CHAPTER 3

WHAT IS A MYSTICAL EXPERIENCE?

I often playfully refer to Mystical Experiences as "the benefits of enlightenment" because they are among the many results of varying degrees of enlightenment.

From my point of view, enlightenment is the *profound personal realization* that *we are all one* and that every event and every thing (which is merely a sustained pattern of events) is both the result of an infinity of causes as well as a partial cause for an infinity of results.

Ultimately, all Mystical Experiences are the direct or indirect result of a person realizing (consciously or unconsciously) that he or she is *one with the universe.*

Although one could potentially identify, segregate, and categorize an infinite number of extremely specific and unique Mystical Experiences, most of them (if not all of them) would qualify as one of six different foundational Mystical Experiences.

The Six Foundational Mystical Experiences are:

1) Healing

I am specifically referring to spiritual/energetic/ emotional/psychological healing; but physical healing is often a direct or indirect and immediate or gradual result. If you have ever experienced this kind of life-changing healing, you know it is possible. If you haven't, you may be skeptical. I believe that the reason this kind of healing is often difficult for many Atheists to initially accept (if they haven't experienced it for themselves) is simply because of the *supernatural* way that it is usually understood and explained. Fortunately, this is a simple matter to resolve. *Keep reading!*

2) Inner Peace

Inner Peace is best described as being a *profound* (not intellectual or conversational) state of acceptance of, and gratitude for, the way everything in the world actually is – especially the circumstances of your own life. The hallmark of genuine Inner Peace is that it is *not dependent* upon one's circumstances. Unfortunately, even for those who have frequently experienced this phenomenon, it can be a difficult state of mind to maintain continuously. Want to know the secret? *Keep reading!*

3) Being in Flow

Being in Flow is known by many names: being in the flow, being in the zone, being on a roll, being visited by Lady Luck, being lucky, being fortunate, being charmed, being blessed by providence, being helped by angels, etc. In every case, the essential experience is the same – feeling supported, assisted, and perhaps even protected; by the universe itself by a means that is not yet fully understood by modern science. Although not well understood, this phenomenon is most certainly *not* supernatural. And anyone can learn to experience it. *This includes you!*

4) Spiritual Ecstasy

Spiritual Ecstasy is known by many names: Awakening within the Dream, Becoming Nothing, Becoming Everything, Union with God, Yoga, Kundalini Awakening, Chakra Explosion, etc. In every case, the essential experience is the same – an expansive, and sometimes explosive, awareness of all that is by a means that is not yet fully understood by modern science. Although not well understood, this phenomenon is most certainly *not* supernatural. And anyone can learn to experience it. *This includes you!*

5) Conscious Intuition

Conscious Intuition is known by many names:

Psychic Intuition, ESP (Extrasensory Perception), Sixth Sense, Second Sight, Telepathy, Clairsentience, Clairvoyance, Clairaudience, Psychometry, etc. In every case, the essential ability is the same – the ability to receive data, knowledge, thoughts, emotions, etc. by a means that is not yet fully understood by modern science. Although not well understood, these phenomena are most certainly *not* supernatural. And anyone can learn to experience them. *This includes you!*

6) Conscious Manifestation

The invisible and invaluable key to Conscious Manifestation wears many different costumes: The Power of Intention, The Law of Attraction, Magic/Magick (all non-illusory forms and spellings), Spell Casting, Incantation, Mantra Chanting, Affirmation Reciting, Prayer, etc. In every case, the essential ability is the same – the ability to influence "reality" by a means that is not yet fully understood by modern science. Although not well understood, these phenomena are most certainly *not* supernatural. And anyone can learn to experience them. *This includes you!*

We will explore all of these potentially life changing Mystical Experiences throughout the remainder of this book; but, first, I want to emphasize two things:

1) As different as all of these experiences may initially seem, they are all made possible by the fact that all things are interconnected (even if only by the

mysterious flow of cause and effect at every level)

2) All of these experiences are made ever more powerful by ever more:

awareness of, acceptance of, and (ultimately) gratitude for universal interconnection ("oneness")

awareness of, acceptance of, and (ultimately) gratitude for anything and everything that one *believes* to be true

Unfortunately, these kinds of experiences of profound awareness, acceptance, and (ultimately) gratitude are always temporary* and, for most people, infrequent,* sometimes to the point of being extremely rare. It is my hope, and my intention, that this book will help make these kinds of experiences much more common, much better understood, and put to much better uses.

---

*Except, perhaps, for those who choose to remain in a near-constant state of meditation, such as the most dedicated monks and mystics of all traditions and no traditions.

CHAPTER 4

HEALING

*In this chapter I am specifically referring to
spiritual/energetic/emotional/psychological healing; but
physical healing is often a direct or indirect
and immediate or gradual result.*

INTRODUCTION

As we live our lives, we experience things that we
accept and things that we *resist*. When we resist, we
create spiritual/energetic/emotional/psychological
(from here on, referred to simply as
"energetic/emotional") injuries.

These kinds of injuries are experienced as resentment,
anger, fear, etc. and are often referred to as "energy
blocks" or "emotional baggage".

A person who generally lives their life continuously
accepting "reality" *in an enlightened and empowered way*

(and thus, lives without an abundance of energetic/emotional injuries) will tend to feel that the entire universe is constantly conspiring to help them in every possible way.

On the other hand, a person who has a difficult time accepting "reality" *in an enlightened and empowered way* (and thus, lives with an abundance of energetic/emotional injuries), will tend to feel exactly the opposite – that the entire universe is constantly conspiring to hinder, or even hurt, them in every possible way.

It is impossible to calculate the full extent to which energetic/emotional injuries negatively affect the quality of one's life, but it is obvious that they do. Even at the most mundane and practical level, there are endless examples that most people have personally experienced and can analyze. Consider how one's resentment, anger, fear, etc. negatively impacts their physical state, psychological state, decision making, actions, interactions, and everything else.

Unfortunately, many people are suffering in significant ways as a direct result of their own energetic/emotional injuries. In order to be free of the endless negative effects of energetic/emotional injuries and begin to enjoy the vast benefits of living without them, energetic/emotional healing is absolutely necessary. *There is no other way!*

Ultimately, energetic/emotional healing is simply a matter of dissolving and releasing one's resistance to "reality" in all of its various forms (resentment, anger, fear, etc.).

In practice, there are innumerable ways to facilitate healing; but, generally speaking, the process is always the same. It is the process of unmasking, identifying, and acknowledging the injury;* followed by the process of finally accepting, forgiving (if necessary), and releasing all of the apparent facts/truths relating to it *forever*. But just because it is easy to understand, doesn't mean it is easy to do.

It is important to understand that *no one* can heal another. *All healing is actually self-healing.* Even in modern physical healing with doctors, surgeries, and medications; it is the body that ultimately has to heal itself.

This being understood, it is equally important to fully appreciate the value of a true healer who knows that their true role is to *facilitate* the life changing process of complete acceptance of truth and complete release of resistance to it. While it is true that an external healer is technically unnecessary; on a practical level, they are essential for many people.

It is also important to understand that the profound experience of healing that I am describing cannot be forced.** It can only arise when the conditions are right. It will then land on the palm of your outstretched hand like a butterfly, but fly away the moment you grasp for it. *This holds true for all Mystical Experiences!*

Fortunately, this experience can be understood and worked towards.

*To be more accurate for the benefit of advanced practitioners, note that unmasking, identifying, & acknowledging are only necessary if one *believes* that they are necessary – and most do.

**Unless, as pointed out in more detail in the introduction of this book, one engages in certain drug use or extreme physical & mental practices. If you are interested in these methods, please seek genuinely experienced and trusted experts in these areas.

THE LESSON

You can't change the truth. You can't change anything that has ever happened; you can't change anything that just now (already) happened; and you will never be able to change anything that will ever happen in the future (once it has happened). In fact, we call the truth "the truth" simply *because* it cannot be changed.

Those things that may or may not happen, but have not yet happened, are simply possibilities (often experienced as hopes and fears); they are not truth and should not be treated as such. Of course, the *presence* of hopes and fears (and any other emotion, thought, etc.) is a very important part of what is true. In other words, if you are afraid that something might happen (or might not happen), it is true that you are afraid and it is true that your fear will be a *partial* cause of whatever will become true in the future.

When we experience the truth as being something other than what we would prefer, we either accept it as it is and make the best of our circumstances; or we resist the truth and demand that it change, often by attempting to make someone (or something) feel badly about themself (fabricating blame, shame, and guilt) in a vain attempt to coerce the truth to change. *But the truth will not be changed!*

When we accept truth as it is, we do not create energetic/emotional injury to ourselves. But when we resist truth as it is, we create energetic/emotional injury to ourselves. Injury which, if we are lucky, we will later have an opportunity to resolve through the process of "healing".

If you find yourself confused (or possibly even irritated) by metaphysical healers', teachers', and others' use of the word "energy", then just substitute the word "emotion" and you will go a long way towards understanding what they are talking about. It doesn't completely capture it, but the essence is there.

For instance, an "energy block" can also be thought of as "emotional baggage". Either way, releasing the block or dropping the baggage is your key to healing!

Fortunately, there are an endless number of creative and valid healing methods, processes, and paths that can lead to this extremely valuable outcome. Choose whatever path feels most comfortable to you and don't worry about what feels most comfortable to others.

With this attitude in mind, I would like to offer a personal healing meditation that I have developed and used over the years while working with clients. It has proven to be extremely effective if undertaken seriously.

THE WORK

How to Heal Yourself

First, put yourself in a comfortable and relaxed posture that you can enjoy for an extended period of time. Then, take a few deep breaths and get as comfortable and as relaxed as you possibly can while staying awake and alert.

When you are ready, begin to review your own life experience; working backwards from the present moment towards your birth (and potentially, beyond). For each memory that arises, notice if there is anything about the memory that makes you feel any unhappiness (as defined in chapter 5). If there is, complete the following process as seriously and sincerely as possible:

1) Notice the difference between the facts you honestly believe to be true and those you are not actually sure of.

2) Decide to accept all that is true as being true, simply because it is true. You don't have to approve of it or be happy about it; just accept that which is true as being true.

3) Decide to allow all that is true to be true, simply because it is true and does not require your permission to be true. Again, this does not mean that you approve of it or are necessarily happy about it; just that you are, perhaps finally, allowing that which is true to be true. *In other words, you are finally surrendering to the truth!*

4) Decide to forgive everyone (including yourself) and everything (whether *apparently* living or not) that had anything to do with causing the truth to be true. Work through this process as necessary. (Want to know the biggest and most powerful secret to forgiveness? Read part II of this chapter! But don't skip ahead just yet!)

5) Decide to send a personal blessing to everyone (including yourself) and everything (whether *apparently* living or not) that had anything to do with causing the truth to be true. This blessing should, at the very least (you can be as elaborate as you like), be an absolutely sincere wish that the recipient may be able to experience anything and everything that he or she wishes in this life and beyond. Be sure not to include any conditions or restrictions. And, of course, be sure to include yourself in this very important distribution of well wishes!

6) Verify that there is no more negative energy to release, no more emotional baggage to drop. Then, feel the deep inner sense of relief, lightness, and brightness that is growing stronger and stronger with your every breath and your every energetic/emotional

release.

Repeat this powerful process as necessary* until you feel little to no negativity about any aspect of your life. Allow yourself to enjoy your ever-lighter sense of being. *And let yourself become filled with ever-greater joy for every reason you can think of, and possibly, for every reason you can't!*

*This process may take hours, days, months, or even years. And just when you think you are finally finished, you may be sorely reminded that there is even more work to be done. This is not a problem. It is simply the truth. And it is the key to your freedom. If you get stuck along the way, please seek help from a trusted healing professional. *It may, initially, be a bit uncomfortable to do this, but it is far beyond worth it!*

How to Help Others Heal Themselves

If you would like to help heal others, there are many modalities available to you. Some of the more currently common examples are Shamanism, Reiki, EFT, Hypnosis, and Personal Counseling (in many forms); but there are many more if you look for them. Choose the path that feels right/best to you and don't worry about what others think of your decision.

Whatever path you choose, it will be extremely helpful to always remember that even though it may or may not be immediately obvious, all modalities work in the same way - by facilitating a process of acceptance, forgiveness, and release. In the end, the fact/truth of the cause of suffering remains, but the energetic/emotional injury itself and its negative effects are gone.

It will also be helpful for you to know that you will be an infinitely more effective and efficient healer if you personally experience and maintain authentic unconditional love of, and for, all that is.

Unconditional love is a living embodiment of truth-seeing, truth-accepting, truth-allowing, and truth-blessing (desiring the best for one and all). In my opinion, true unconditional love is actually the single most powerful energetic/emotional healing modality there is or can ever be. *Imagine a world wherein everyone naturally understood and lived in true love. Imagine!*

If you genuinely try to live your life as an unconditional loving witness of all that is true (regardless of what is true), you will gradually find that you will radiate in profound ways and that others will be drawn to you (consciously and unconsciously). And as you genuinely witness, love, and bless (desire the best for) others; they will begin to allow themselves to genuinely witness, love, and bless themselves (and others) – and healing will begin to happen naturally and spread naturally from one person to others, ad infinitum.

Mysteriously, you will even find that your entire body *really does radiate*. You will feel energy coursing to your body, through your body, and from your body. It will make the short hairs on your body stand on end. It will cause warm (and sometimes hot or even cold) sensations to arise and flow through your body. And you will feel as though you are being filled, healed, and empowered by something profound and indescribable. And you will come to realize that *whatever it is,** it allows you to both heal yourself and help others heal themselves in ways that will never cease to amaze you.

Just like the well-known healers throughout all of time; you, too, can become a living embodiment and example of unconditional love. And if you want to become a truly great healer (known or unknown), you will.

---

*It is known by many names: Universal Life Force Energy, Reiki, Ki, Qi, Prana, The Breath of God, The Spirit of God, God's Love, *Unconditional* Love, *True* Love, etc.

Part II: FORGIVENESS
There is only Innocence

Unfortunately, in our present day and age, a chapter on healing would be incomplete if it didn't specifically address the topic of forgiveness.

First, I would like to state that the idea of forgiveness is a mistake. Ultimately, it is an absurdity.

As thoroughly explained in my previous book entitled *Spiritual Atheism – The Way of Wisdom*, my position is that, *technically*, there is no "free will". From my perspective, the idea of forgiveness is based upon what I consider to be a very serious misunderstanding (belief in "free will").

The need for forgiveness necessarily implies the belief that someone or something (whether *apparently* living or not) could have (technically, not theoretically) done something other than what they/it did, and that what they/it did was inherently and absolutely (as opposed to contextually and relatively) wrong.

Said less accurately, but more simply, the need for forgiveness implies the belief that someone could have *literally* done something other than what they did *and* that what they did was *inherently and absolutely wrong*.

As one begins to understand, internalize, and integrate an ever more accurate understanding of the nature of the infinite and eternal flow of cause and effect at every scale, this view (the erroneous belief expressed above) can only evoke deep tears of compassion for all who still hold it and for all who interact with them.

Blame, shame, and guilt all rely upon the imaginary "gift" of "free will" in order to establish their validity. If nothing and no one could ever have done anything other than what it/he/she has done, is doing, and will do, then what is there to forgive?

I want to strongly affirm my position that all of life, including every human being that has ever lived or will ever live, is absolutely and scientifically innocent. *Ultimately, there is only innocence!*

For more information about my perspective of "free will", please see my previous book entitled *Spiritual Atheism – The Way of Wisdom*

What About Accountability?

Accountability does *not* disappear along with the idea of "free will", blame, shame, guilt, etc.

First, we are all part of the one universe and none can escape the natural flow of cause and effect.

Secondly, any time a society organizes itself at any level, "codes of conduct" begin to emerge that are (hopefully) intended to nurture the health and happiness of and for all (individually and collectively, including environment, etc.). Within such a society, accountability is entirely relevant, important, and not at all in conflict with the nature of nature (wherein "free will" does not, *technically*, exist). Rather, it is an expression of it!

This, however, does not mean that the members of any specific society will be endowed with any particular degree of wisdom in their creation and enforcement of such codes. And it should be emphatically stated that no good can result from making someone feel badly about their actions, no matter how heinous, even if they are asked, requested, obliged, and/or forced to "make things right".

Now that I have brought up the idea of "right" and "wrong"...

I would like to suggest that "right" (aka "good") simply refers to that which nurtures greater well-being, and "wrong" (aka "evil") simply refers to that which nurtures lesser well-being.* Of course, this kind of judgment depends upon the point of reference (the perspective of the one(s) making the judgment); the scale of self identity;** and the degree of intelligence, knowledge, and wisdom available and applied. *Among other things!*

I see "right" and "wrong" as entirely relevant and important (but largely misunderstood) judgments that have nothing to do with the inherent innocence or imaginary guilt of a person, place, or thing. Instead, I see the judgment of "right" and "wrong" as simply one's *best attempt* to determine whether the outcome(s) of a thought, decision, action, etc. will be (or were) more likely to nurture greater or lesser well-being.

In my opinion, the world needs wise judgment, wise

codes, and wise enforcement. *Systems, however, are unlikely to be wiser than their creators, and very likely to be significantly less!*

*For more information, please refer to my previous book entitled *Spiritual Atheism – The Way of Wisdom* (See Appendix III: Wholistic Ethics)

**Presently, Earth makes a nice practical wholistic identity. Of course, considering how much space exploration we are doing and how much space trash we are creating, we really should start thinking about our *practical* wholistic identity as being our entire solar system. *Naturally, as our interaction, influence, and impact expands, our sense of wholistic identity will continue to expand.*

CHAPTER 5

INNER PEACE

INTRODUCTION

Inner Peace is the natural result of living life in such a way that one *continuously* accepts (does not resist) one's assessment of the truth *in an enlightened and empowered way*.

It is also the natural result of an effective healing process, as described in the previous chapter.

Naturally, after finally arriving at a place of authentic Inner Peace through an effective healing process; one typically has an inherent desire to follow the path that offers prevention (acceptance of one's perception of "reality") rather than the path that continually requires a new cure (resistance to one's perception of "reality").

It is often said that an ounce of prevention is worth a

pound of cure. In my opinion, this common adage is an incredibly serious understatement - at least when it comes to one's own health and happiness!

Following the "path of prevention" is not only an *extraordinary investment* in one's health and happiness; it also offers some amazing and potentially unexpected gifts such as the natural development of increased healing powers (for self and others), Inner Peace (potentially to the point of Spiritual Ecstasy), Conscious Intuition, and Conscious Manifestation.

As mentioned in Chapter 3, Inner Peace is best described as being a *profound* (not intellectual or conversational) state of acceptance of, and gratitude for, the way everything in the world actually is – especially the circumstances of your own life. The hallmark of genuine Inner Peace is that it is *not dependent* upon one's circumstances.

For this reason, I think of "Inner Peace" as *true* happiness. *Common* happiness, on the other hand, is 100% dependent upon one's circumstances. In other words, people commonly experience Inner Peace only when *certain things* are true; but enlightened people generally experience Inner Peace *no matter what* is true.

It is also important to point out that Inner Peace is experienced on a sliding scale (based primarily on gratitude), meaning that it can range from a neutral feeling of profound peace, to feeling like you are living "in the flow" with the entire universe conspiring to support you, to an explosive feeling of orgasmic union with all that exists.

In any event, Inner Peace is the key to experiencing Being In Flow, Spiritual Ecstasy, Conscious Intuition, and Conscious Manifestation (of whatever you desire). For this reason, I think of Inner Peace as the most beneficial, or the most fortunate, state of mind. For this same reason, your top priority (after healing) should be to protect, maintain, and nurture Inner Peace in any and every circumstance in which you find yourself.

That being said, it is important to understand that the profound experience of Inner Peace that I am describing cannot be forced.* It can only arise when the conditions are right. It will then land on the palm of your outstretched hand like a butterfly, but fly away the moment you grasp for it. *This holds true for all Mystical Experiences!*

Fortunately, this experience can be understood and worked towards.

*Unless, as pointed out in more detail in the introduction of this book, one engages in certain drug use or extreme physical & mental practices. If you are interested in these methods, please seek genuinely experienced and trusted experts in these areas.

THE LESSON

Let's explore some foundational principles.

First, it is critical to understand that all beings desire to be personally happy above all else. All other desires represent what one *believes* will cause ever-greater personal happiness.

If you are willing to be absolutely honest with yourself while you analyze any situation carefully, you will find that even the most complicated and supposedly selfless desires can be quickly reduced to an underlying desire to be personally happy.

This is fundamental. This cannot be changed. This is not a problem.

Rather than attempting to defend selflessness and altruism, it would be far more productive to seek to fully understand and apply this (and all) truth to our lives.

It is meaningful to describe happiness as the result of (one's perception of) "reality" being in alignment with one's desires; however, happiness is actually more accurately understood as being the result of one's (conscious and unconscious) *requirements for happiness* being met by (one's perception of) "reality".

You see, desires actually come in two different forms: Requirements and Preferences.

Requirements are desires that you have (consciously or unconsciously) *decided are required* for your happiness. Requirements are risky because they put your happiness (Inner Peace) at risk. If your requirements are not met or are otherwise violated; you have decided that unhappiness is not only the natural result, but that it is also fully justified!

From my perspective, you should never put your Inner Peace at risk.

A simple example would be, "If you don't come to dinner with me, I am going to be extremely unhappy!"

Preferences, on the other hand, are desires that you are consciously aware of, and that you have *consciously decided are not required* for your happiness. Preferences are the only safe desires because, if sincere, they do not put your Inner Peace at risk.

As I have said, from my perspective, you should never put your Inner Peace at risk.

A simple example would be, "It would be great if you can join me for dinner; but, either way, I am going to do my best to enjoy myself immensely."

With desires that are preferences, as opposed to requirements, it is entirely possible to experience Inner Peace (fundamental happiness) and still feel that "reality" is not in alignment with one's desires (which, in this case, are preferences rather than requirements).

True happiness is the result of truly accepting, and authentically appreciating to whatever degree is possible, (one's perception of) "reality" – even if it isn't in alignment with one's preferences. This is the key to Being In Flow, Spiritual Ecstasy, Conscious Intuition, and Conscious Manifestation (of whatever you desire).

Unhappiness is the exact opposite experience. It is resistance, sometimes violent, to (one's perception of) "reality"; and it is the key to energetic/emotional injury, emotional and physical pain and illness, patterns of continuous victimization, and a generally hellish life experience. If you want to avoid these things, you must learn to monitor and master your own state of mind. It may be a difficult habit to form, but it is essential to your happiness!

It is of the highest importance that you realize that if you are experiencing any moment in a state of mind other than that of Inner Peace; then you are, in fact, injuring yourself. Such an injury will become a candidate for later healing.

Similarly, if you experience any moment in a state of true, conscious, and deep Inner Peace; no energetic/emotional injury can result. In such a case, there will be no need for later energetic/emotional healing related to that moment.

Therefore, I suggest that you actively attempt to master the art of living every moment as authentically peacefully (happily) as possible.

To this end, I would like to offer a personal living meditation that I have developed and used over the years while working with clients. It has proven to be extremely effective if undertaken seriously. Master it for yourself and then teach it to everyone you can - especially children. The sooner these habits are formed, the better life will be; both for the individual possessing them and for everyone around them.

THE WORK

How to Maintain a State of Inner Peace

Do your best to be totally present in every moment of your life. Be aware of what is true here and now, wherever and whenever you are. Also, be aware of your desires for the near and/or long term future, because your desires are also part of what is true.

Then, be in a state of mind wherein you are absolutely committed to seeing, accepting, and allowing whatever you discover to be true, to be true. You don't have to be (and can't truly be) happy about the things that you are not happy about, but realize and practice the wisdom of accepting the truth as it is and allowing it to be as it is.

Make sure that you really do want to see and know the truth. Make sure that you really are committed to honoring the truth by accepting it as the truth. Make sure that you really do feel a state of allowing it to be as it is so that there is not a trace of resistance within you.

Then, attempt to make the very best and the very most of each and every moment by doing the following three things *simultaneously*:

1) Accept and allow all that is true to be true. Remember, you can't change historical truth.

Resistance is futile... and personally damaging!

2) Appreciate everything you can about what is true.
Fake appreciation will bring fake results. It's ok if there is very little you are presently able to authentically appreciate; but you should know that there is always something and it is in your best interest to discover and celebrate it. If nothing else, appreciate the fact that you are still breathing. If even that it is not something you can authentically appreciate; then actively appreciate the fact that, eventually, you won't be (breathing).

3) Actively nurture the manifestation of whatever you would prefer to be true in the near and/or long term future.

Know your preferences and your priorities, but be careful not to create any requirements. Affirm that you strongly prefer, *but do not require*, whatever it is that you desire (prefer). Then, do everything you *want* to do, to make your dreams (preferences) come true.

That's it!

Of course, I do fully realize that living every moment in this way is much easier said than done. Nonetheless, if you will practice this living meditation long enough, then you will eventually discover that you can, in fact, allow yourself to be supremely happy *simply because you can!*

Ultimately, you are the judge and jury of your own happiness; so, if possible, lower your own requirements for happiness until there is only *the requirement of existing!*

"I exist, therefore I am supremely happy!"

THE KEY TO UNHAPPINESS
Fear and Resistance

What is unhappiness?

For the purposes of this book, unhappiness refers to a state of mind that is generally characterized by the following (or similar) qualities:

afraid, angry, blaming, closed, cold, complaining, confused, conniving, controlling, cruel, cynical, defensive, depressed, disconnected, discouraged, disempowered, dishonest, dissatisfied, distrustful, fearful, forceful, guilting, hateful, impatient, inflexible, irritable, jealous, mean, manipulative, negative, ornery, paranoid, pessimistic, powerless, resistant, restless, sad, shaming, stingy, suspicious, tense, tight, tyrannical, unloving, unlucky, ungrateful, uninspired, victimized, worried, etc.

Naturally, one in an unhappy state of mind will not necessarily experience all of these qualities at the same time, but they do tend to enjoy each other's company immensely. Thus, to the unconscious and unhappy person comes even more unhappiness - and quickly!
People commonly believe that they are unhappy because certain undesired things have happened. From my point of view, an opposite proposal is far more accurate (and useful): undesired things tend to happen (much more frequently) when a person is unhappy.

For this reason, I often refer to unhappiness as the *unfortunate (or victimized)* state of mind.

What is the cause of unhappiness?

Unhappiness arises when one resists what one perceives to be, or believes to be, true; and is greatly intensified if one refuses to accept truth and allow it to be true. Ultimately, the greater the resistance, the greater the unhappiness.

So... if you want to feel really, really authentically unhappy, simply focus all of your attention on those things that you most wish were different than they presently are and increase, as much as possible, your resistance to accepting and allowing the truth to be as it appears to be! Let yourself feel as resistant, bitter, angry, sad, depressed, etc. as you possibly can!

And learn this lesson well!

THE KEY TO HAPPINESS
Love and Acceptance

What is happiness?

For the purposes of this book, happiness refers to a state of mind that is generally characterized by the following (or similar) qualities:

accepting, allowing, appreciative, calm, confident, connected, courageous, ecstatic, encouraged, empowered, faithful, fearless, flexible, forgiving, fortunate, generous, grateful, happy, honest, inspired, kind, loving, lucky, open, optimistic, patient, playful, peaceful, powerful, relaxed, satisfied, trusting, warm, etc.

Naturally, one in a happy state of mind will not necessarily experience all of these qualities at the same time, but they do tend to enjoy each other's company immensely. Thus, to the conscious and happy person comes even more happiness - and quickly!

People commonly believe that they will be happy when certain desired things happen. From my point of view, an opposite proposal is far more accurate (and useful): desired things tend to happen (much more frequently) when a person is happy.

For this reason, I often refer to happiness as the *fortunate (or empowered)* state of mind.

What is the cause of happiness?

Happiness is the natural result of accepting and allowing that which is true to be true. The less resistance you have to the truth, the happier you will feel. And the more authentic appreciation and gratitude you have for what you believe to be true, the deeper your happiness will be.

So... if you want to feel really, really authentically happy, simply focus all of your attention on those aspects of your life, and life in general, that you are the most genuinely grateful for and increase, as much as possible, your appreciation for those things! Let yourself feel as peaceful, appreciative, happy, fulfilled, ecstatic, etc. as you possibly can!

And learn this lesson well!

CHAPTER 6

BEING IN FLOW

INTRODUCTION

Have you ever felt like you woke up on the "wrong" side of the bed? Like almost everything that happened to you on that particular day went wrong, or was otherwise generally unfortunate? Tragically, this feeling can sometimes last for days, weeks, months, or even years.

Being in Flow is the exact opposite experience. It is the feeling of waking up on the "right" side of the bed. Like almost everything that happens goes right, or is otherwise generally fortunate. Just like its polar opposite, this feeling can last for days, weeks, months, or even years.

As explained in Chapter 3, Being in Flow is known by many names: being in the flow, being in the zone, being on a roll, being visited by Lady Luck, being lucky, being fortunate, being charmed, being blessed by providence, being helped by angels, etc. In every case, the essential experience is the same – feeling supported, assisted, and perhaps even protected, by the universe itself by a means that is not yet fully understood by modern science.

It is important to understand that the profound experience of Being in Flow that I am describing cannot be forced.* It can only arise when the conditions are right. It will then land on the palm of your outstretched hand like a butterfly, but fly away the moment you grasp for it. *This holds true for all Mystical Experiences!*

Fortunately, this experience can be understood and worked towards.

*Unless, as pointed out in more detail in the introduction of this book, one engages in certain drug use or extreme physical & mental practices. If you are interested in these methods, please seek genuinely experienced and trusted experts in these areas.

THE LESSON

The experience of Being in Flow is the natural result of having no resistance to (your perception of) "reality" while being simultaneously fully engaged with it. The experience of Being in Flow is amplified in direct relationship to your level of realization that emerging "reality" is actually responding to your own personal state of mind. *That is, if it doesn't disturb you!*

The experience of Being in Flow...

will usually cause you to become more aware of coincidence and synchronicity.

will usually cause you to become more aware of your internal response to external things.

can sometimes feel peaceful and patient; but, other times, can feel stimulating and urgent.

can sometimes cause you to feel confident; but, other times, can cause you to feel vulnerable.

may cause you to feel as though you are being guided by voices inside of you - *and outside of you!*

may cause you to feel as though the universe, itself, is somehow, in some mysterious way, helping you.

may cause you to feel as though you are somehow, in some mysterious way, influencing emerging "reality".

may cause you to feel a sense of immense possibility and an overwhelming desire to help others feel it too.

may cause you to feel as though, in some mysterious way, you are moving *with* the flow of the universe.

may cause you to feel as though, in some mysterious way, "reality" is actually emerging *with the flow of you!*

Experiencing Being In Flow for even a few moments

(especially if you aren't used to it) can feel as though you have momentarily awakened, at least partially, *within* the dream of life. *Perhaps you have!*

THE WORK

How to get In Flow

To get In Flow as quickly as is possible, simply accept all that is true (as described in previous chapters) and imagine that the entire universe is actually conspiring to help you have the experiences that you want to have, even if you do not feel that way now or understand how it could even be possible.

Remember your fundamental intention to maintain a peaceful and happy state of mind; and your intention to recognize, appreciate, and amplify the greatness in every moment.

Consciously intend to find out how great this moment, the future, and life in general can be.

With this general state of mind, it is *much easier* to experience Being In Flow.

Here are a few simple steps to guide you until this way of living becomes habitual:

1) Affirm your desire (as a preference, rather than requirement) to Be In Flow.

2) In whatever way seems most appropriate and powerful to you, formally invite the entire universe to help you. For many people this begins as a private meditation (or prayer), but it can also be a spoken or written request.

3) Accept and allow all that is true to be true.

4) Appreciate everything you can about what is true.

5) Imagine that entire universe is conspiring to help you experience whatever it is that you desire. Alternatively, imagine that life is actually a dream and that you are (one of) its dreamer(s).

6) Be fully *present* in the continuously emerging moment. Let go of everything that concerns you (any and every source of resistance) and trust that the universe will guide, direct, and otherwise help you experience whatever it is that you desire.

7) Be fully *engaged* in the continuously emerging moment. Look for resonances, coincidences, synchronicities, signs, symbols, and anything else that captures your attention. Then, determine if it inspires, empowers, or guides you in any way. Get immersed in this exercise with profound awareness. Just as an athlete, musician, artist, etc. can get in the zone by focusing all of their attention on their game, performance, creation, etc.; you can get In Flow by focusing all of your attention on your game – the game of life and living!

8) Actively discover how great each passing moment

can be by actively making it as great as you can.

9) Finally, remember that the experience of Being In Flow cannot be forced and may not happen for you. The good news is that if you can *genuinely* accept this without disturbing your Inner Peace, your success is almost guaranteed. *Eventually.*

How to stay In Flow

The best way to stay In Flow is simply to stay fully present and engaged in the continuously emerging moment without resisting or clinging to anything in any way. Know that the feeling of Being In Flow can arise as quickly as it can disappear. Accept that fact and appreciate Being In Flow when the experience arises. Allow it to come and go as it pleases - *again, like a butterfly landing on your outstretched hand!*

How to get back In Flow

If you have been enjoying the experience of Being In Flow and you suddenly find yourself feeling as though you have drifted out of flow, do not be distressed. This is natural.

Being In Flow is like basking in the Sun. Clouds come and clouds go. Allow the weather to be as it is while accepting, appreciating, and enjoying, to the fullest extent possible, whatever weather is present.

Try focusing all of your attention on those things that

have the qualities you want more of. And, of course, re-read "How to get In Flow" (found earlier in this chapter). Also, keep notes about your own experiences; so that, over time, you can create your own personal, and ever more powerful, process for getting back In Flow and staying In Flow.

And when the Sun finally does shine again, embrace and engage it with all you've got; knowing and accepting (with absolutely no resistance) that it could, again, be obscured by clouds at any moment.

Such is life!

CHAPTER 7

SPIRITUAL ECSTASY

INTRODUCTION

As explained in Chapter 3, Spiritual Ecstasy is known by many names: Awakening within the Dream, Becoming Nothing, Becoming Everything, Union with God, Yoga, Kundalini Awakening, Chakra Explosion, etc. In every case, the essential experience is the same – an expansive, and sometimes explosive, awareness of all that is by a means that is not yet fully understood by modern science.

Spiritual Ecstasy is the ultimate progression of the experience of Inner Peace (having absolutely no resistance to what appears to be true) and Being In Flow (living as though life is a dream and you are (one of) its dreamer(s)).

Gradually (sometimes rapidly), one's experience of Inner Peace and Being in Flow becomes so strong that one begins to progressively realize (consciously and/or unconsciously) that they are actually one with all that is - *in an extremely intimate and most mysterious way!*

Spiritual Ecstasy in its most progressed form is the ultimate experience of *awakening within* the dream of life. There are no more concepts. There are no more others. There is only the overwhelmingly ecstatic experience of *existing and being!*

To be clear, Spiritual Ecstasy is a temporary (ranging from extremely short-lived to indefinitely enduring) psychological and physical climactic experience.

Compared to (typical) sexual ecstasy, Spiritual Ecstasy can be exponentially more profound, explosive, satisfying, and lasting. That being said, it is possible to experience both simultaneously – an experience unlike any other!

Unfortunately, for most people, Spiritual Ecstasy is a rare experience. The problem is that, like all Mystical Experiences, it is very difficult to demonstrate on demand. If one's "preference" that the experience occur has even a hint of "requirement", it simply cannot happen – at least not to any great degree. This is because having *no resistance* to what is true is one of its causes. For this reason, Spiritual Ecstasy most often occurs when it is not intended at all.

It is important to understand that the profound experience of Spiritual Ecstasy that I am describing cannot be forced.* It can only arise when the conditions are right. It will then land on the palm of your outstretched hand like a butterfly, but fly away the moment you grasp for it. *This holds true for all Mystical Experiences!*

Fortunately, this experience can be understood and worked towards.

*Unless, as pointed out in more detail in the introduction of this book, one engages in certain drug use or extreme physical & mental practices. If you are interested in these methods, please seek genuinely experienced and trusted experts in these areas.

THE LESSON

Naturally, all experiences of Spiritual Ecstasy are unique, but most often they tend to share some similar qualities. What follows is an *example* of such an experience.

Imagine that at some point you find yourself feeling profoundly peaceful, accepting, appreciative, generous, open, etc. Then, suddenly and unexpectedly, your short body hairs stand on end as energetic waves of pleasure* begin to wash through your body and mind.

It feels as though these energetic waves of pleasure* are actually cleansing and healing your body and mind by dissolving or transmuting any existing energetic/emotional injury.

And as your body and mind becomes ever more purified and healed, they become ever more capable of receiving ever more of this pleasurable,* purifying, healing, and empowering energy.

If you can stay objective, allowing, and open (rather than subjective, grasping, and judging), this experience may (there are an innumerable number of factors involved) continue to compound and magnify until you lose all sense of your individual self and feel as though you are united with all that exists. You may even feel as though you *are* all that exists.

At this point, your body may be stiff, fluid, vibrating, or moving in unexpected ways. Sometimes, this experience can feel very similar to a sexual orgasm, except that this experience generally involves your entire body in a much more comprehensive and much less sex organ oriented way.

As with sexual orgasm, this experience can become so strong, so powerful, so consuming; that it would be unbearable if you were trying to bear it. Of course, the best course of action is to let go (in every way, at every level, consciously and unconsciously) and allow your body and mind to be vulnerable to, and manipulated by, this naturally overwhelming experience.

If you are fortunate (again, there are an innumerable number of factors involved), it will seem as though this *mysterious energy,*** now unblocked and unstopped, is radiating through your body and mind like light through a light bulb.

If you are even more fortunate, it will seem as though

you have *awakened within* the dream of life, as described above.

This is an example of the profound experience of Spiritual Ecstasy. Naturally, your experiences of Spiritual Ecstasy may be different.

Ironically, this *rare experience* is the natural result of (an admittedly profound level of) awareness of the only experience that *always is* – that of existing and being.

Also note that the depth of your experience of Spiritual Ecstasy is in direct relationship to the depth of your innermost authentic gratitude and love for everything as it is. *Authentic gratitude and love is the inverse of resistance!*

---

*Depending upon how much injury is still within you, the wave of energy may be initially experienced as painful. But don't be alarmed, these experiences will eventually become immensely pleasurable. Perhaps not during your first or second such experience, but eventually. *Hang in there and let the healing happen!*

**It is known by many names: Universal Life Force Energy, Reiki, Ki, Qi, Prana, The Breath of God, The Spirit of God, God's Love, *Unconditional* Love, *True* Love, etc.

THE WORK

The more authentically peaceful you are on a continuous basis, the more likely it is that you will experience Spiritual Ecstasy. *So, maintain your Inner Peace!*

Also, remember that the experience of Spiritual Ecstasy cannot be forced (except as previously footnoted) and may not happen for you. The good news is that if you can *genuinely* accept this without disturbing your Inner Peace, your success is almost guaranteed. *Eventually!*

With these things in mind, let's get started.

You will be resting in one position for as many hours as you desire, so you've got some important choices to make:

1) Choose comfortable clothes. Sometimes it's nice to have a soft warm blanket, too.

2) Choose a private and comfortable location. Be sure to turn off phones, tablets, computers, and other potential sources of disturbance. If indoors, don't forget to close the curtains and bolt the doors (as appropriate).

3) Choose a comfortable and sustainable place to rest. Some options include: directly on bare earth, on a floor, pillow, cushion, chair, stool, table, bed, etc.

4) Choose a comfortable and sustainable posture.

Some things to consider about posture:

I don't believe that any particular posture is *required*, but I do believe that certain postures (especially straight and symmetrical postures) make having the experience much more likely and potentially much more intense.

Not surprisingly, I find the traditional lotus position (feet resting on the legs) while sitting on the bare earth to be the most powerful option; but, unfortunately, I can't personally sustain it. Therefore, I tend to use the modified lotus position (feet resting on the ground) while sitting on a cushion. Also, I have had similar experiences (although admittedly not quite as strong) while sitting with straight and symmetrical posture on a soft chair. I've even had them while laying on a bed in a "Vitruvian Man" (the famous drawing of the outstretched man by Leonardo da Vinci) posture.

Probably the most important thing is that your chosen posture can be sustained long term (even if eventually painful) and that it won't encourage you to become drowsy or, even worse, fall asleep.

Yep, snoring is a definite buzz kill!

Once you have carefully considered and made your choices, it is time to begin the actual work.

THE ACTUAL WORK

1) Sit in your chosen posture without moving for as long as desired. My most powerful experiences have occurred after several days of relatively continuous work.

2) Get your mind right:

a) Affirm your *preference* to experience Spiritual Ecstasy *and accept that you may not experience it!*

b) If you do begin to experience it, allow it and witness it without grasping for it or clinging to it.

c) Maintain an open heart. If you are resisting anything, you cannot experience union with everything.

d) Be an accepting, allowing, and loving witness of your perception of truth.

3) Allow your mind to do as it does while you carefully observe it and become ever more keenly aware of it. At this point, your awareness should be focused strictly on remaining aware of your mind's stream of thoughts. Ignore all other sensory input.

4) If you can stay aware of your mind's stream of thoughts without resisting (or otherwise reacting) to them, eventually your mind will begin to calm down. This may take more time than you would prefer. Be patient.

5) Once your mind has calmed down and the time feels right, actively direct your mind's attention to its own awareness of the feeling of its own existence. This is an expansive awareness of the always present feeling of existing itself; it is not an intellectual inquiry or understanding. At this point, your mind should be in a state of awareness only, rather than in a state of thinking. You will know that the time is right because

your attempts to complete this step will be more an act of requesting and guiding than of coercing and forcing.

6) Do your best to remain in an objective state of awareness only as your mind ever more narrowly and ever more precisely experiences its own existence. Allow whatever you experience to develop and grow in its own way and in its own time.

7) When you feel ready, release your every last trace of resistance to truth (known and unknown) and surrender all that you are to all that is. Give yourself explicit permission to disintegrate and be absorbed into infinite oneness. Allow the result of your complete and profound surrender to be whatever it will be.

8) At some point, whatever you are experiencing may begin to suddenly swell and explode into a profound and potentially indescribable experience. If this happens, don't panic or cling to your experience; just keeping breathing as seems natural at the time and allow it to be as it is. Eventually, your amazing experience will subside and you can consider it.

9) You may have an experience that seems completely different from anything I have described or hinted at in this book. If so, again, don't panic or cling to your experience; just keeping breathing as seems natural at the time and allow it to be as it is. Eventually, your unique experience will subside and you can consider it.

An additional note of potential interest to some: I once had the experience of feeling a massive presence of "energy" coming from outside of my body and impacting my body bluntly and explosively, and then coursing and spreading through my body like a watery fire. In this extreme case, I could literally feel the lingering physical results of the experience in my body for several days – perhaps even longer. (I wonder if I just got used to the new feelings?)

BONUS POINTS

I'm sure you can imagine that if you happen to be able to share this experience with a partner who is also having this experience, it would be a phenomenal time to make love. You might even turn into pure light and physically disappear, taking the whole world with you. *Who knows?!*

CHAPTER 8

CONSCIOUS INTUITION

INTRODUCTION

Have you ever realized that you knew something that you had no identifiable way of knowing? Perhaps you asked yourself a question and could hear the answer like a whisper coming from within your own mind. Or perhaps you had a dream that you later realized was actually a premonition. Or perhaps you looked at something or someone (or a photo of the same) and suddenly had a random flash of insight about that something or someone that turned out to be true.

These are just a few different examples of how Conscious Intuition can manifest itself in daily life.

As explained in Chapter 3, Conscious Intuition is known by many names: Psychic Intuition, ESP (Extrasensory Perception), Sixth Sense, Second Sight, Telepathy, Clairsentience, Clairvoyance,

Clairaudience, Psychometry, etc. In every case, the essential ability is the same – the ability to receive data, knowledge, thoughts, emotions, etc. by a means that is not yet fully understood by modern science.

Unfortunately, Conscious Intuition (in all of its various forms) is often falsified to varying degrees (for varying reasons), which makes it extremely tempting for most critical thinkers to dismiss it altogether. But for those who have personally had such an experience, there can be no doubt that the ability to receive knowledge, thoughts, emotions, etc. by a means that is not yet fully understood by modern science can and does actually exist.

The problem is that, like most Mystical Experiences, it is very difficult to demonstrate on demand. This is because there are many factors involved; many of which can not be effectively controlled on demand, and many more that have not yet been identified and are not yet understood.

Also note that Conscious Intuition often brings knowledge of mundane occurrences, circumstances, situations, etc. that goes unnoticed altogether. In these cases, extraordinary opportunities to gain valuable insights might either be taken for granted or missed altogether because they weren't recognized for what they actually were. Most people are simply not aware of their inherent ability to know things, regardless of whether we are talking about significant or insignificant things.

Fortunately for you, you now have a conscious

choice: you can choose to ignore your inherent ability to know things; or you can choose to embrace and invest the time and energy required to learn to create the conditions required for ever-greater awareness, so that you can enjoy the benefits of Conscious Intuition as you navigate your life journey.

It is important to understand that the profound experience of Conscious Intuition that I am describing cannot be forced.* It can only arise when the conditions are right. It will then land on the palm of your outstretched hand like a butterfly, but fly away the moment you grasp for it. *This holds true for all Mystical Experiences!*

Fortunately, this experience can be understood and worked towards.

---

*Unless, as pointed out in more detail in the introduction of this book, one engages in certain drug use or extreme physical & mental practices. If you are interested in these methods, please seek genuinely experienced and trusted experts in these areas.

THE LESSON

If you have gone through the healing process described in Chapter 4 (the more times the better) and are earnestly trying to live every moment according to the wisdom shared in Chapter 5 (don't worry, perfection isn't possible or necessary), you will find that Conscious Intuition naturally occurs much, much more frequently – *that is, if you are making an active effort to become ever more aware of it!*

Why? Because when your mind stops creating and clinging to pain and fear (stops resisting your perception of the truth of the past, present, and future), it begins to experience everything in an ever-less biased and pre-conditioned way.

Biases prevent one from sensing, seeing, hearing, etc. the truth clearly. It can be like pulling a blanket over ones eyes in order to not see what is there. Or, even worse, it can be like additionally projecting one's hopes and fears onto the blanket in an effort to try to change the truth - or at least fool one's self and/or others.

This kind of pain and/or fear based blindness (denial) and imagination (projection) seriously impedes and distorts one's natural Conscious Intuition.

On the other hand, if one has a fearless desire to know, accept, appreciate, and maximize *whatever is true*, even in the face of potential pain; they will be actively searching for and authentically open to all knowledge – even if it appears to threaten their current beliefs, desires, etc.

Ultimately, there are two basic keys to ever-greater Conscious Intuition:

1) The deep and authentic desire to know what is true *above all else*, along with the continually demonstrated ability to accept and appreciate truth without resisting it.

2) The practice of ever-increasing one's *conscious* awareness of one's *subtle* awareness – in any and every form.

The following process has been designed to support these two basic intentions.

THE WORK

As always, do your best to make sure that you feel no resistance to the truth, and therefore enjoy a relatively constant state of Inner Peace.

Also, remember your intention to recognize, appreciate, and amplify the greatness in every moment. Finally, remember your intention to find out how great this moment, the future, and life in general can be.

With this state of mind, you can become extremely intuitive. Here are a few simple steps to guide you until this way of living becomes habitual.

How to Increase your Conscious Intuition

1) Affirm your desire (as a preference, rather than a requirement) to *know* that which will help you live a healthy and happy life, and help you help others live a healthy and happy life.

2) In whatever way seems most appropriate and powerful to you, formally invite the entire universe to help you. For many people this begins as a private

meditation (or prayer), but it can also be a spoken or written request.

3) Stop "doing" as often as possible and for as long as possible in order to actively "listen" for any new information that might be within your field of awareness, but not yet formally recognized and considered.

Start by looking around and noticing what you notice. If anything captures your attention, ask yourself why and what it might mean to you – metaphorically or otherwise. Listen for an answer. If none comes after a few minutes, continue on to whatever else captures your attention.

Do the same thing with your ears. Listen to everything you can hear and carefully explore whatever captures your attention.

Do the same thing with all of your other senses: smell, taste, and touch. For instance, ask yourself: How does the air smell? What do you notice about it? How does the air taste? What do you notice about it? How does the air feel? What do you notice about it? Be poetic. Be free.

Finally, after exploring all of your mundane senses, begin to explore your inner mind's senses. Ask yourself: What am I aware of that I haven't yet noticed? Listen deeply. Be patient. Be an extremely careful and critical observer.

If you have the time and interest, you could "listen"

for hours, days, months, or years and find that there is no end to what you are actually aware of at some level. In fact, if you practice sincerely enough and long enough, you will, at some point, realize that you need only form a question and you will begin to "hear" (sense) the answer.

4) Always follow your intuition, whether it makes sense to your conscious mind or not. The more you accept, allow, and trust life; the more strongly you will be guided by a "still small voice" from within. Perhaps it is your own innermost voice. Perhaps it is the voice of life itself. Perhaps there is no difference. In any event, *trust it!*

4a) That being said, don't let go of your discernment! If something feels wrong (bad or harmful), it probably is wrong. (Note that if something feels new, unfamiliar, or scary; it isn't necessarily wrong.) Also, never follow any other person's judgment if it is in opposition to your own, unless you have an extremely good reason for doing so (which does sometimes happen). *Always use your best judgment and you will naturally sharpen your skills as you find your way!*

4b) If you find it difficult to determine the difference between genuine intuition and mental or emotional chatter (false intuition), the following insights may help you:

Mental chatter is an experience of imagination and *rationalization* that is fed by conscious or unconscious hopes and/or fears. *Genuine intuition is an experience of knowing, without justification.*

Emotional chatter is an experience of imagination and *emotionalization* that is fed by conscious or unconscious hopes and/or fears. *Genuine intuition is an experience of knowing, without emotional persuasion.*

5) If, at any point, you find that you are not presently in a state of authentic inner peace (in other words, you have any difficulty accepting anything that is true), reread chapters 4 and 5 of this book.

6) Actively and authentically recognize and appreciate anything and everything that nurtures your health, your happiness, and anything else that you desire.

7) Constantly ask yourself the question: "How can I (not how *could* I, but how *can* I) make this moment even better for myself and for those around me?" And then, if possible, do it!

8) Ultimately, seek to answer, with your very life itself, the most powerful question of all: "How great can my life be?"

It's your life! Make it an ever-better one!

CHAPTER 9

CONSCIOUS MANIFESTATION

There is great wisdom in being resistless to the truth while simultaneously remaining aware of your personal preferences for the not-yet-manifested future. Personal preferences, however, are not demands placed upon the universe. Nor are they requirements for happiness.

INTRODUCTION

Conscious Manifestation is the experience of becoming, being, having, or doing something you desire.

Have you ever absent-mindedly wished that something would happen and then been dumbfounded when things turned out almost exactly as you had wished? Or perhaps you can think of a time when you more thoughtfully focused your thoughts, words, and actions on a particular desire until it became a "reality"? Or perhaps you actively practice a very technical form of pagan or occult magic? Or perhaps you, or someone you know, uses prayer to great effect?

These are just a few different examples of how people Consciously Manifest specific experiences.

As explained in Chapter 3, the invisible and invaluable key to Conscious Manifestation wears many different costumes: The Power of Intention, The Law of Attraction, Magic/Magick (all non-illusory forms and spellings), Spell Casting, Incantation, Mantra Chanting, Affirmation Reciting, Prayer, etc. In every case, the essential ability is the same – the ability to influence "reality" by a means that is not yet fully understood by modern science.

Unfortunately, the ability to Intentionally Manifest (regardless of which method one chooses to use) is often falsified to varying degrees (for varying reasons), which makes it extremely tempting for many critical thinkers to dismiss altogether. But for those who have personally had such an experience, there can be no doubt that the ability to manifest specific desired experiences can and does actually exist.

The problem is that, like most Mystical Experiences, it is very difficult to demonstrate on demand. This is because there are many factors involved; many of which can not be effectively controlled on demand, and many more that have not yet been identified and are not yet understood.

Also note that Conscious Manifestations often come

by way of mundane occurrences, circumstances, situations, etc. that go unnoticed altogether. In these cases, extraordinary opportunities to fulfill one's desires might either be taken for granted or missed altogether because they weren't recognized for what they actually were. Most people are simply not aware of their inherent ability to manifest, regardless of whether we are talking about significant or insignificant circumstances and experiences.

The hidden-in-plain-sight secret is that you are *always* manifesting and cannot do otherwise. So, it is either from an ignorant, unconscious, and unintentional place or an enlightened, conscious, and intentional place.

Fortunately for you, you now have a conscious choice: you can choose to ignore your inescapable ability to manifest, or you can choose to embrace it and invest the time and energy required to master it; *but*, you cannot choose to *not* manifest anymore than you can choose to *not* be part of the universe. We are one and the same.

That being said, it is important to understand that the profound experience of Conscious Manifestation that I am describing cannot be forced.* It can only arise when the conditions are right. It will then land on the palm of your outstretched hand like a butterfly, but fly away the moment you grasp for it. *This holds true for all Mystical Experiences!*

Fortunately, this experience can be understood and worked towards.

*Unless, as pointed out in more detail in the introduction of this book, one engages in certain drug use or extreme physical & mental practices. If you are interested in these methods, please seek genuinely experienced and trusted experts in these areas.

THE LESSON

Manifestation (whether conscious and intentional or unconscious and unintentional) is the result of one's unconscious state. Therefore, the sometimes elusive key to Conscious Manifestation is actually the unconscious mind.

The deepest level of the unconscious mind does not have its own intentions. It simply has a state of being that is reflective of one's conscious and unconscious perceptions, beliefs, desires, intentions, etc.

For this reason, the most mystical methods of Conscious Manifestation are primarily ways to manipulate one's own unconscious mind rather than the world around them.

It may not always be obvious at first glance; but if you study any given method long enough, you will eventually discover that the real mystical secret of its success is that if you can change the state of your unconscious mind, you can change the way you experience and interact with the world around you. (For instance, even on the most mundane level, you may start to notice things that were always there, but were previously dismissed as insignificant or went unnoticed altogether.)

To be absolutely clear, if you intend to Consciously Manifest, your first (and in some cases, *only*) endeavor should be to influence your unconscious mind.

As stated above, this is the true agenda and real secret to all authentic methods of Conscious Manifestation. The rest of the process is just good-old-fashioned mental and physical work, as required.

In summary, the mystical key to Conscious Manifestation is to create and maintain a *stable* state of conscious *and* unconscious acceptance of and gratitude for:

> your perception of "reality" (whatever it may be)
> *This is non-resistance and the key to your power.*

> your preferred "reality" (imagined as "reality")
> *This is the seed and pattern for your manifestation.*

FOUR IMPORTANT WARNINGS:

Remember that, for our purposes, "good" is simply that which contributes to wholistic health and happiness, and "evil" is simply that which contributes to wholistic disease and unhappiness.

1) Be careful what you wish for; you just might get it... and perhaps a few other unanticipated consequences as well!

2) Know that guidance and assistance will show up for any and every intention, regardless of whether it is a "good" or "evil" intention.

3) Know that the qualities of whatever intention you create and send out into the world will be received and amplified most effectively by your own unconscious mind. Nurture "evil" intentions and you will tend to have more "evil" experiences. Nurture "good" intentions and you will tend to have more "good" experiences.

4) Finally, know that you will very likely underestimate the extent to which your intentions affect yourself, others, and the world around you. For this reason, it is extremely wise to always make sure that your intentions are conditionally similar to: "I wish for ... , as long as it will not detract from the highest good of all". Rest assured, your innermost intentions *do* have an impact on all that is; so, please, use your ever-increasing power wisely. *With great power comes great responsibility!*

It may be helpful to frequently ask yourself these kinds of questions while listening very carefully for answers:

In what ways might my desired manifestation help my self or any other person, place, or thing be genuinely healthier and/or happier?

In what ways might my desired manifestation cause harm to my self or any other person, place, or thing?

Will it cause more help than harm?

Will the help and/or harm be long term or short term? How long or short term?

Will the help and/or harm continue to spread on it's own (via cause and effect) or will it be limited in scope? How limited?

Indeed, there are many natural incentives for actively monitoring and purifying your intentions. The depth of your purity is the depth of your alignment with all that nurtures wholistic health and happiness.

With this in mind, I'd like to share with you a very powerful way to influence the nature of emerging "reality".

THE WORK

As always, do your best to make sure that you feel no resistance to the truth, and therefore enjoy a relatively constant state of Inner Peace.

Also, remember your intention to recognize, appreciate, and amplify the greatness in every moment. Finally, remember your intention to find out how great this moment, the future, and life in general can be.

With this state of mind, you can cause very powerful positive changes in your own life and in the world around you. Here are a few simple steps to guide you until this way of living becomes habitual.

How to Increase your Conscious Manifestation

1) Reread the FOUR IMPORANT WARNINGS included above and then clarify exactly what effects you want to cause (your ultimate intention). Then, personally commit to *doing* whatever is required, for as long as is required, in order to nurture the manifestation of your ultimate intention - *even if it requires the rest of your life! (if appropriate)*

2) In whatever way seems most appropriate and powerful to you, formally invite the entire universe to help you. For many people this begins as a private meditation (or prayer), but it can also be a spoken or written request.

3) In every moment, accept and allow all that is true to be true. (as described in previous chapters)

4) In every moment, do everything you can to nurture the manifestation of your preferred "reality".

Over the years, I have created a couple of practical and powerful ideas that have been very helpful to some. I refer to them as the "The Six 'P's of Perspective" and "The Four 'E's of Effort".

The Six "P"s of Perspective:

Be Peaceful. Accept "reality", whatever it may be, forever.

Be Positive. Believe that everything is leading, eventually, to your desired result.

Be Prioritized. Know what is most important for *you* to be doing *now*.

Be Persistent. Know that if you give up, your desired result is given up.

Be Patient. Know that impatience almost always leads to either a significantly distorted version of your desired result or complete failure.

Be Powerful. Know that your Perspective is your Power.

The Four "E"s of Effort:

Generally, your thoughts, words, and actions should be as **Ethical, Effective, Efficient,** and **Enjoyable** as is possible.

5) Always follow your intuition, whether it makes sense to your conscious mind or not. The more you accept, allow, and trust life; the more strongly you will be guided by a "still small voice" from within. Perhaps it is your own innermost voice. Perhaps it is the voice of life itself. Perhaps there is no difference. In any event, *trust it!*

Also, look for resonance, coincidence, and synchronicity; which are all signs of Being In Flow.

6) If, at any point, you find that you are not presently in a state of authentic inner peace (in other words, you have any difficulty accepting anything that is true), reread chapters 4 and 5 of this book.

7) Actively and authentically recognize and appreciate anything and everything that nurtures your health, your happiness, and anything else that you desire.

8) Constantly ask yourself the question: "How can I (not how *could* I, but how *can* I) make this moment even better for myself and for those around me?" And then, if possible, do it!

9) Ultimately, seek to answer, with your very life itself, the most powerful question of all: "How great can my life be?"

It's your life! Make it an ever-better one!

CHAPTER 10

HOW TO LIVE YOUR BEST LIFE

Now that you know how to: heal yourself and others, live peacefully and happily, get in flow and stay in flow, experience bliss and ecstasy, gain knowledge intuitively, and wield endless power; *what's next?*

What's next is for you to take your new knowledge, apply it to your life, practice it every day, and...

find out how great YOUR life can be!

Unfortunately, I cannot tell you that you will now go on to live the life that you think *you want to live*; but I can tell you that if you will invest the time and energy required to apply this new knowledge to your life, you will get to live the very best life that *you can live.*

The truth is that we do *not* all have *equal* opportunities in life. Some people do have an easier time with fewer challenges, more natural abilities and resources, and more rewards; while others have a more difficult time with more challenges, fewer natural abilities and resources, and fewer rewards.

Such is life!

Fortunately, if I have been successful, the information contained in this book will contribute significantly to the positive causes that affect your life experience. It is now up to you to *decide* how you want to feel, what you want to know, and how much creative power you want to wield in the world. *You have been enlightened!*

That being said, I do understand that many readers of this book will require additional guidance in order to fully understand and master these teachings.

In addition to my other related books and articles; I offer courses and other events (offline and online), along with a very limited amount of private sessions.

There are also many other good healers, teachers, courses, and books available. Use your intuition and choose the healers, teachers, courses, and books that feel most resonant and empowering to you.

I can not directly express how much your personal and individual health and happiness means to me; but, if you have understood the essence of what I am attempting to share with you in this book, *you know.*

May you live in peace, flow, bliss, and ecstasy with all of the knowledge and power you desire!

.

APPENDIX

ABOUT ENLIGHTENMENT

I hesitate to include this potentially confusing, discouraging, and/or agitating (for some) information here; but, eventually, it becomes extremely helpful to understand (or have confirmed). For this reason, I have decided to accept the inherent risks of sharing this information for the benefit of those who are ready for it and/or are seeking it. Please read this appendix last!

Are Spiritual Atheists "enlightened"?

Anyone who has enough insight to refer to themself as a "Spiritual Atheist" is almost certainly on a path that leads to enlightenment; but, naturally, not all who are on such a path will stop long enough to evaluate the evidence that is always all around (and within) them. The truth is always here. *Stop and observe it!*

What is enlightenment?

From my point of view, enlightenment is the *profound personal realization* that we are all one and that every event and every thing (which is merely a sustained pattern of events) is both the result of an infinity of causes as well as a partial cause for an infinity of results. Ultimately, from my point of view, enlightenment includes (among other things) the realization that, *technically*, there is no "free will" at any level.

About "Free Will"

It seems important to first point out that it is very often most appropriate and most powerful to use language that implies choice (particularly when describing things on a *practical* level). I have written this book with this in mind.

That being said, make no mistake, the greatest tragedy of all time is the erroneous assumption of "free will".

Ironically, those who come to truly understand and embrace this most empowering *technical* truth will, on a *practical* level, gain an ever-greater ability to influence the emerging dream of ever-changing existence.

Unfortunately, most people are *extremely attached**** to their belief in "free will" and are, therefore, extremely unlikely to ever realize this most empowering *technical* truth. Those that do learn will very likely experience a natural grieving process that may include varying levels of denial, anger, sadness, acceptance, and (finally) peace; before they can begin to enjoy the benefits of this most empowering *technical* truth.

Then, finally, the chains that bind such an awakening person will become the tools that serve them, and they will live in a constant state of mystical awe. In the meantime, such a person should pay extremely close attention to the relationship between their attachment to their belief in "free will" and their attachment to their sense of "self".

For more information about my perspective of "free will", please see my previous book entitled *Spiritual Atheism – The Way of Wisdom*

*My inner conspiracy theorist sometimes imagines that the promotion of "free will" is (or was originally) an intentional effort to keep the most empowering truth hidden from the masses. You know, *"Let's make the people believe that they are free so that we can more easily control them with blame, shame, and guilt and ultimately prevent them from discovering their own true power! Muhaha!"*

About the Mundane and Mystical "Self"

All awareness arises from the capability of a body (thing) to be aware.

Ultimately, I am both my body (including any ever-subtler bodies, if such exists) and its awareness.

Similarly, you are both your body (including any ever-subtler bodies, if such exists) and its awareness.

I *am,* and you *are,* most narrowly identified as *awareness only*. Ultimately, I *am,* and you *are,* a *witness only*. Neither I nor you can truly *originate* anything.

Indeed, in a very profound (and potentially disturbing to some) way, all sufficiently sophisticated bodies (or ever-subtler bodies) are simply "robots" that have been "programmed" by an infinity of things.

Awareness, however, is much more mysterious.

About "Reality", the Dream, and Awakening

I refer to (all-inclusive) **ever-changing existence** as "reality" (in quotes). I also refer to it as *the dream.*

It is not actually possible to wake up *from* the dream of ever-changing existence. This is because that which facilitates your awareness exists *within* ever-changing existence and not outside of it. It is, however, possible to wake up *within* the dream of ever-changing existence.

To be *ever more awake within the dream* means to be *ever more aware of the nature of ever-changing existence (and your relationship to it) and ever more present in each continuously emerging moment .**

Note that every conscious being is a part of the universe that has become conscious; and every such being can (potentially) become ever more awake and, thus, (potentially) become an ever more powerful influencer of "reality" (the dream).

It is important to point out that all that exists, whether conscious or not, is simultaneously, *but not equally*, influencing "reality" (the dream). Therefore, we should treat each other as existential equals, while realizing that we may not be equal in any other way. *Wisdom with compassion is the way of the awakened!*

---

*One of the most profound and powerful ways to become ever more aware of the nature of ever-changing existence (and your relationship to it) and ever more present in each continuously emerging moment, is to meditate in a truly empowering way. Only by becoming deeply aware of *nothing* can one experience the profound awareness of *everything*. Said differently, awareness *seems to be* inherently infinite and eternal; but thought *seems to* inherently limit and shape awareness.

OTHER BOOKS BY SOREN SORENSEN

Spiritual Atheism
The Way of Wisdom

Spiritual Atheism is no oxymoron. It is the key to your happiness. And it is the key to a better world. This book will challenge you to reconsider your foundational philosophical assumptions about the nature of existence, identity, motivation, happiness, healing, forgiveness, free will, consciousness, creation, intention, and manifestation from a shockingly direct and extremely powerful point of view. Discover a radical, inspiring, and liberating way to understand your life and live it to its *fullest potential!*

A Book That Could Change the World
Confessions of a Spiritual Atheist

This magickal book presents a progressive series of simple, yet cryptic, confessions (beliefs) that are each accompanied by a playful and symbolic illustration. Each idea invites an intriguing inquiry into the beliefs, assumptions, and attitudes that shape your life experiences; causing an ever-greater expansion of consciousness and intention that is sure to change your world, and the world around you, *for the better!*

For more information about these and other books, please visit: www.SpiritualAtheistWisdom.com

ABOUT THE AUTHOR

SOREN SORENSEN

Soren Sorensen has been promoting Spiritual Atheism for more than 30 years. Soren is the creator of the Center for Spiritual Atheism as well as the Center for a Better World. He is also the author of several books about Spiritual Atheism and teaches related courses and offers supportive coaching to his students.

Soren has been serving as a spiritual teacher, healer, counselor, and life coach since 2005, after leaving his successful 10-year career as a systems analyst. He chose to make "helping people" the central focus of the next phase of his life's work after receiving overwhelming feedback from co-workers and friends that his insights, questions, and suggestions were changing their lives.

Soren has the rare ability to guide his clients on a direct and compassionate exploration of their personal life experiences that quickly shatters the illusions that are keeping them from their own happiness and power to create positive changes in their own lives and in the world around them.

Like many natural philosophers before him, Soren has been fascinated by the nature of existence since early childhood, and he continues to refine his perspective through careful observation, meditation, and experimentation.

For more information, please visit:
www.SpiritualAtheistWisdom.com

CPSIA information can be obtained
at www.ICGtesting.com
Printed in the USA
LVHW100433070723
751612LV00002B/311